MW00950959

LOW SUGAR SNACKS

For information contact IronRingPublishing.com

ISBN-13: 978-1523798773

ISBN-10: 1523798777

First Edition: February 2016

10 9 8 7 6 5 4 3 2 1

Foreword

by Dan DeFigio, author of
Beating Sugar Addiction
For Dummies
BeatingSugarAddiction.com

Obesity and diabetes are at an all-time high. Sugar overload is a driving force behind obesity, diabetes, liver disease, auto-immune disorders, chronic fatigue, and metabolic syndrome. It has become my mission to help guide and educate the public with sound nutrition and exercise advice. Part of that mission is working with those who promote similar goals, and that's why I wanted to offer my support for Mary Donovan's collection of **Low Sugar Snacks** recipes.

Snacking Tips For Diabetics

An important part of blood sugar control is eating often enough. Snacks are an important way for diabetics to help keep blood sugar levels more stable throughout the day. Here are a few pointers for stabilizing blood sugar levels:

1. Protein and fat reduce your insulin response to carbohydrates. An all-carb snack is a poor choice for those who struggle with high blood sugar levels. Be sure to include protein and/or fat every time you eat!

2. Don't eat too much at one time. Small portions will result in lower blood sugar spikes – and fewer calories consumed.

3. Be sure to drink enough water throughout the day. Diabetics often develop kidney problems, and keeping the water flowing will help keep your kidneys healthy. Drinking enough water will also keep you from getting dehydrated and having your brain turn on the craving signals.

4. Stay away from diet drinks! Artificial sweeteners are bad for your brain, and they disrupt your normal hunger and full signals. Instead, try mineral water flavored with fresh citrus, or some herbal tea.

Table of Contents

COOKED LOW-SUGAR SNACKS

Chicken Skewers

Yield: 8 servings

Ingredients

1 Tablespoon fresh dill, chopped

1 Tablespoon fresh chives, chopped

1 Tablespoon fresh parsley, chopped

1 Tablespoon coconut oil

3/4 teaspoon onion powder

3/4 teaspoon garlic powder

3/4 teaspoon paprika

Salt and pepper
12 ounces chicken breast, skinless, boneless,
cut into 1-inch pieces

2 medium sweet peppers, cut into 1-inch pieces

1 cup fresh snow pea pods, whole

Directions

1. Prepare skewers, preferably 6" long, by soaking in water for 30 minutes (if made of wood).
2. Combine all spices and herbs in a bowl.

3. Add chicken, sweet peppers and snow peas. Mix to coat evenly with spices and herbs.
4. Arrange alternate pieces of chicken, sweet peppers and snow peas through skewers.
5. Grill for about 10 minutes over medium heat. Chicken should no longer be pink.

Nutrition Information

Serving size: 2 skewers
Calories: 63
Total Fat: 18 g
Total Carbohydrate: 3 g
Sugars: 2 g
Protein: 7 g
Sodium: 100 mg

Mediterranean Carrot Dip

Yield: 16 servings

Ingredients

1 cup carrots, chopped

1 15-ounce can garbanzo beans, rinsed and drained

1/4 cup tahini

2 Tablespoons lemon juice

2 cloves garlic, peeled and sliced

1/2 teaspoon cumin

Salt and pepper

1 Tablespoon fresh parsley, chopped

Vegetable sticks

Directions

1. Cook carrots in boiling water until tender, then drain.
2. Puree carrots along with garbanzo beans, tahini, lemon juice, garlic, cumin, and salt in a food processor or blender.
3. Place puree in a small bowl. Add parsley and stir.
4. Chill for at least 1 hour before serving as a dip with your favorite vegetable sticks.

Nutrition Information

Serving size: 2 Tablespoons
Calories: 60
Total Fat: 2 g
Total Carbohydrate: 8 g
Sugars: 1 g
Protein: 2 g
Sodium: 124 mg

Seasoned Kale Chips

Yield: 6 cups

Ingredients

8 cups curly kale, rinsed and dried, broken into pieces (no stems)

1 Tablespoon olive oil

1 teaspoon lemon juice or apple cider vinegar

Salt and pepper

Directions

1. Combine oil and lemon juice in a large bowl.
2. Add kale and toss to coat with oil and juice.
3. Sprinkle with salt and pepper. Toss to coat evenly.
4. Lay Kale in single layers in baking sheets.
5. Bake in a preheated oven at 350-400 °F, watching closely, for about 10 minutes.
6. Chips are done when crisp.

Nutrition Information

Serving size: 1 cup
Calories: 65
Total Fat: 3 g
Total Carbohydrate: 9 g
Sugars: 2 g
Protein: 3 g
Sodium: 119 mg

Baked Onion Rings

Yield: 2 servings

Ingredients

1 medium onion, sliced into half-inch-thick rings
Ice water (enough to cover onion rings)
1/2 cup bread crumbs
2 egg whites

Directions

1. Preheat oven to 400 degrees F.
2. Soak onion rings in ice water.
3. Dip the rings in egg whites followed by the breadcrumbs.
4. Bake for about 20 minutes at 400 F.
5. Onion rings are done when nicely browned.

Nutrition Information

Serving size: 1 serving
Calories: 168
Total Fat: 1.6 g
Total Carbohydrate: 30 g
Sugars: 6.7 g
Protein: 8.4 g
Sodium: 257 g

Crispy Spiced Zucchini Chips

Yield: 14 servings

Ingredients

Salt and pepper
A pinch of cayenne
A pinch of thyme
A pinch of rosemary
1 large zucchini, sliced thinly

Directions

1. Preheat oven to 400 degrees F.
2. Combine salt and spices in a bowl.
3. Toss zucchini slices into seasoning, coating evenly.
4. Spread slices in a baking tray and bake for about 20 minutes until crisp.

Nutrition Information

Serving size: 1 serving (about 20 chips)
Calories: 15
Total Fat: 0.1 g
Total Carbohydrate: 3.6 g
Sugars: 1.5 g
Protein: 0.6 g
Sodium: 77 mg

Seafood and Rice Salad

Yield: 8 servings

Ingredients

2 cups cooked brown rice, chilled
1 cup cooked wild rice, chilled
2 tins or 6 ounces smoked mussels
1/2 cup red bell pepper, diced
1/2 cup yellow or green bell pepper, diced
1 cup cucumber, peeled and diced
3 Tablespoons light mayonnaise
3 Tablespoons light sour cream
1 Tablespoon fresh dill, chopped
1 Tablespoon fresh lemon juice
1/4 teaspoon freshly ground pepper

Directions

1. In one mixing bowl, combine rice, mussels, bell peppers, and cucumbers, mixing well.
2. In a second mixing bowl, whisk together the rest of the ingredients.
3. Toss contents of second bowl into rice mixture.
4. Serve.

Nutrition Information

Serving size: 1 serving (about 2/3 cup)
Calories: 159
Total Fat: 5 g
Total Carbohydrate: 22 g
Sugars: 2 g
Protein: 7 g
Sodium: 114 mg

Apple Muffins

Yield: 12 muffins

Ingredients

1 1/4 cups oat bran cereal, uncooked
1 cup whole wheat flour
2 teaspoon ground cinnamon
1 teaspoon baking powder
3/4 teaspoon baking soda
1/2 teaspoon salt
3/4 cup unsweetened applesauce
1 cup apple, peeled, cored, diced
1/4 cup honey
1/2 cup vegetable oil
1 medium egg
1 teaspoon vanilla extract
Non-stick cooking spray

Directions

1. Coat muffin pans with non-stick cooking spray of line with muffin liners
2. Preheat oven to 375 º.
3. Prepare 2 bowls, medium for dry and large for wet ingredients.
4. Combine cereal, cinnamon, baking powder, baking soda, and salt in one bowl.

5. Combine applesauce, honey, oil, egg and vanilla in the large bowl. Gradually add dry ingredients while stirring.
6. Add diced apple and stir.
7. Pour batter into muffin cups up to about ¾ full.
8. Bake for 15-20 minutes. Muffins are done when a toothpick inserted in the center comes out clean.

Nutrition Information

Serving size: 1 muffin
Calories: 120
Total Fat: 7 g
Total Carbohydrate: 18 g
Sugars: 2.7 g
Protein: 3 g
Sodium: 107 g

Flourless Cheese Muffins

Yield: 12 small muffins

Ingredients
6 eggs (beaten)
1/2 cup almond meal
1/2 cup oat flakes (blended)
1/2 cottage cheese (low fat)
1/2 cup parmesan cheese (finely grated)
1/4 cup flax seed meal
1/3 cup finely chopped scallions
1/2 tsp. baking powder
Seasoning to taste

Directions
1. Preheat oven to 375 degrees F.
2. In a large bowl add almond meal, oat flakes, parmesan cheese, flax seed meal, baking powder and seasoning to taste. Mix well.
3. Mix the chopped scallions with the eggs. Add to dry mixture. Combine well.
4. Spoon the mixture into silicone muffin molds.
5. Bake 20-30 minutes until edges brown.

Nutrition Information

Serving size: 1
Calories: 197
Total fat: 14.5 g
Total carbohydrates: 11.2 g
Sugar: 0.8 g
Protein: 11.6 g
Sodium: 0.29 g

Almond Apple Muffins

Yield: 12 muffins

Ingredients
4 eggs (beaten)
2 cups almond meal
1 cup apple sauce (unsweetened)
5 scoops protein powder
4 Tablespoons butter
1/2 Tablespoon cinnamon

Directions
1. Preheat oven to 350 degrees F.
2. Melt butter in the microwave.
3. In a bowl, mix the rest of the ingredients.
4. Add butter. Mix again.
5. Spoon the mixture into muffin molds.
6. Bake 15-20 minutes.

Nutrition Information
Serving size: 1
Calories: 233
Total fat: 16.7 g
Total carbohydrates: 7.5 g
Sugar: 3.0 g
Protein: 13.1 g
Sodium: 0.16 g

Garlic-Parmesan Sticks

Yield: 12 servings

Ingredients
13.8 ounces pizza dough
3/4 cup Romano or goat cheese (shredded)
3/4 cup Garlic and Herb cream cheese (low fat)
1/4 cup Parmesan cheese
1/2 tsp. freshly chopped oregano

Directions
1. Preheat over to 400 degrees F.
2. Roll out dough to 12-inch square.
3. Cover baking pan with parchment paper. Place the dough.
4. Bake 10 minutes.
5. Remove from oven. Spread Garlic and Herb cream cheese, Romano/goat cheese, and parmesan cheese. Sprinkle freshly chopped oregano.
6. Put back in oven and bake 15 minutes.
7. Slice into 12 pieces.

Nutrition Information
Serving size: 2 sticks
Calories: 135
Total fat: 5 g
Total carbohydrates: 17 g
Sugar: 1 g
Protein: 6 g
Sodium: 0.4 g

Potato Puffs

Yield: 18 puffs

Ingredients
2 egg whites
1 cup mashed potatoes
1/2 cup chopped broccoli
1/4 cup parmesan cheese (finely shredded)

Directions
1. Preheat oven to 400 degrees F.
2. In a medium mixing bowl, mix mashed potatoes with broccoli, half the parmesan cheese, and 2 egg whites.
3. Spoon mixture evenly into 18 cupcake molds.
4. Top with remaining parmesan cheese.
5. Bake 20-25 minutes.

Nutrition Information
Serving size: 1 puff
Calories: 23
Total fat: 0.8 g
Total carbohydrates: 2.1 g
Sugar: 0.3 g
Protein: 1.9 g
Sodium: 56.2 mg

Mocha Cream Puffs

Yield: 20 cream puffs

Ingredients
4 ounces vanilla yogurt (low-fat)
4 ounces light whipping cream (lightly whipped)
3 whole eggs
3/4 cup flour
3/4 cup water
3 Tablespoons butter (softened)
2 Tablespoons cocoa powder (raw, unsweetened)
2 tsp. coffee crystals
1/8 tsp. salt

Directions
1. Preheat oven to 400 degrees F.
2. In medium saucepan, combine water, butter, 1 Tablespoon coffee crystals, and salt. Bring to a boil.
3. Reduce heat to simmer. Add flour and stir continuously for about 5 minutes until a ball forms.
4. Add eggs one at a time. Whisk until well-combined.
5. Divide dough into 20 balls and place on paper lined baking pan.
6. Bake 25 minutes at 400 degrees F.
7. Filling: Combine vanilla yogurt, cocoa powder, and remaining coffee crystals.

8. Fold in lightly-whipped desert topping. Chill for 15 minutes.
9. Cut the puffs in half and scoop the soft dough from inside.
10. Fill with chilled cream using a spoon.

Nutrition Information

Serving size: 1 puff
Calories: 66
Total fat: 4.5 g
Total carbohydrates: 4.8 g
Sugar: 1 g
Protein: 1.8 g
Sodium: 108.1 mg

Parmesan Crackers

Yield: about 30 crackers

Ingredients
6 ounces whole wheat flour
4 Tablespoons butter
2 ounces cornmeal
2 ounces parmesan cheese (finely shredded)
2 ounces skim milk
1 tsp. baking powder
Dash of salt
Dash of cayenne pepper

Directions
1. Preheat oven to 375 degrees F.
2. In a large bowl, combine all of the ingredients and form a dough.
3. Wrap in plastic and set to rest for 15-20 minutes.
4. Roll the dough to 1/8 inch thickness.
5. Cut out little crackers into desired shape.
6. Line on a baking pan lined with paper and bake for 5 minute minutes at 375 degrees F.
7. Flip over the crackers and bake for another 4-5 minutes.
8. Remove from oven and cool completely before serving.

Nutrition Information
Serving size: 1 cracker
Calories: 46
Total fat: 2 g
Total carbohydrates: 5.8 g
Sugar: 0.1 g
Protein: 1.7 g
Sodium: 128.9 mg

Cheesy Tomato Bruschetta

Yield: approx. 22 servings

Ingredients
1 French whole wheat baguette
2/3 cup cream cheese (low fat)
3/4 cup tomatoes (chopped)
1/3 cup shredded spinach
2 Tablespoons olive oil
1 tsp. fresh oregano (finely chopped)

Directions
1. Preheat oven to 425 degrees F.
2. Cut the baguette into thin slices.
3. Sprinkle olive oil on both sides of each slice.
4. Place on a baking pan lined with paper. Bake 10 minutes.
5. While bread is baking, combine cream cheese with oregano in a small bowl.
6. Remove baguette slices from the oven. Spread cream cheese mixture evenly on each baguette slice.
7. Top with tomatoes and spinach.

Nutrition Information

Serving size: 1 bruschetta
Calories: 38
Total fat: 2.5 g
Total carbohydrates: 2.7 g
Sugar: 0.3 g
Protein: 1.2 gr
Sodium: 36.6 mg

NO-COOK
LOW-SUGAR
SNACKS

Fruit and Nut Balls

Yield: about 20 balls

Ingredients

1 cup fruit (like mango, strawberry, peach, kiwi, banana, apricots, etc.), pureed

1 cup desiccated coconut (plus extra to coat later)

3/4 cup traditional oats

2 Tablespoons nuts (cashew, peanut, hazelnut, walnuts, almonds, etc.), crushed

2 Tablespoons coconut oil or rice bran oil

2 teaspoons carob powder (optional)

Directions

1. Blend ingredients together in a blender to desired texture. Mix until mixture begins to stick together. You may add more oats and nuts if mixture is too moist.
2. Scoop the mixture with a Tablespoon to form balls.

3. Sprinkle the extra desiccated coconut on a shallow tray or plate. Coat the balls by rolling over the coconut.
4. Serve.

Nutrition Information
Serving size: 1 ball
Calories: 57
Total Fat: 4.5 g
Total Carbohydrate: 4.2 g
Sugars: 0.5 g
Protein: 0.7 g
Sodium: 3 mg

Black Bean and Avocado Salad

Yield: 6 servings

Ingredients

1 15-ounce can black beans, low sodium, rinsed and drained

1/2 cup tomatoes, chopped

1/2 cup celery, chopped

1/2 cup green bell pepper, chopped

1/4 cup avocado, cubed

2 teaspoons lemon juice

1 clove garlic, minced

Salt and pepper

Directions

1. Combine and toss all ingredients together (be careful not to mash the avocado cubes).

2. Serve.

Nutrition Information

Serving size: ½ cup
Calories: 57
Total Fat: 1 g
Total Carbohydrate: 10.6 g
Sugars: 1.3 g
Protein: 4.3 g
Sodium: 79 mg

Apple, Beet and Carrot Salad

Yield: 4 servings

Ingredients

3/4 cup beets, pre-shredded

3/4 cup carrots, pre-shredded

2 cups apple, shredded

1/4 cup walnut halves, chopped

3 Tablespoons parsley, chopped

1 Tablespoon lemon juice

1 Tablespoon olive oil

Salt and pepper to taste

Directions

1. In a large mixing bowl, combine beets, carrots, and apple.
2. Top with walnuts and parsley.
3. In a separate bowl, whisk together lemon juice, salt and pepper to make the dressing.
4. Pour and distribute dressing evenly into the salad.
5. Serve.

Nutrition Information

Serving size: 1 serving
Calories: 112
Total Fat: 8 g
Total Carbohydrate: 11 g
Sugars: 8 g
Protein: 2 g
Sodium: 330 mg

Salsa with Orange and Avocado

Yield: 10 servings

Ingredients

3 cups orange, peeled, chopped

2 1/2 cups pink grapefruit, peeled, chopped (about 2 large grapefruit)

1/4 cup minced red onion

2 Tablespoons chopped fresh cilantro

1 Tablespoon minced jalapeño pepper

2 teaspoons fresh lime juice

1/2 teaspoon kosher salt

1 diced peeled avocado

Directions

1. Combine all ingredients in a bowl. Toss.
2. Serve.

Nutrition Information

Serving size: 1/4 cup
Calories: 86
Total Fat: 3 g
Total Carbohydrate: 14.7 g
Sugars: 2 g
Protein: 1.3 g
Sodium: 98 mg

Melon Ball Cooler

Yield: 6 servings

Ingredients

1/2 cup berry-flavored sparkling water, zero calorie

3 Tablespoons balsamic vinegar

4 cups assorted melon balls

Directions

1. Toss all ingredients gently together.
2. Chill for at least 2 hours.
3. Serve.

Nutrition Information

Serving size: about ¾ cup
Calories: 47
Total Fat: 0 g
Total Carbohydrate: 11 g
Sugars: 9.3 g
Protein: 1 g
Sodium: 16 g

Peanut Butter Jelly Balls

Yield: 6 balls

Ingredients
2 Tablespoons natural peanut butter
2 Tablespoons sugar-free jelly or jam
3 Tablespoons cracker crumbs
1 Tablespoon raw-unsweetened cocoa powder
1/2 tsp. vanilla extract

Directions
1. In a food processor mix the peanut butter, 1 Tablespoon cracker crumbs, cocoa powder, and vanilla extract.
2. Form 6 balls using your hands.
3. Roll the balls into the remaining cracker crumbs.
4. Press a hole with your finger in the middle of each ball and fill it with jelly.

Nutrition Information
Serving size: 1 ball
Calories: 50
Total fat: 3 g
Total carbohydrate: 5 g
Sugar: 1.6 g
Protein: 2 g
Sodium: 56.6 mg

Hummus Dip with Veggies

Yield: Ten 1/4 cup servings

Ingredients
1 can (15.5 ounces) unsalted garbanzo beans
4 ounces water
2 garlic cloves
1/4 cup tahini paste
3 Tablespoons lime juice
2 Tablespoons olive oil
Salt and pepper to taste

Directions
1. Place beans and garlic into food processor. Pulse 5-6 times.
2. Add water, tahini, lime juice, olive oil, salt and pepper.
3. Blend until smooth.
4. Serve with carrots, celery, broccoli, peppers, or other fresh vegetables of choice.

Nutrition Information
Serving size: 1/4 cup
Calories: 52
Total fat: 2.4 g
Total carbohydrate: 6 g
Sugar: 1 g
Protein: 2 g
Sodium: 0.3 g

Blueberry Yogurt Frozen Bites

Yield: 10 servings

Ingredients
1 cup blueberries (around 125)
1 cup fat-free vanilla yogurt (no added sugar)
1 Tablespoon stevia powder

Directions
1. Mix the vanilla yogurt with stevia.
2. Add blueberries. Mix again.
3. Place blueberries on a paper lined tray using a fork.
4. Freeze for an hour.
5. Store in the freezer.

Nutrition Information:
Serving size: 12-13 blueberries
Calories: 27
Total Fat: 0.1 g
Total Carbohydrates: 5.4 g
Sugar: 4.4 g
Protein: 1.1 g
Sodium: 1.5 mg

Peanut Butter Yogurt Dip with Apples

Yield: 6 servings

Ingredients
5 sliced apples
3 cups Greek yogurt (low-fat)
1/2 Tablespoon honey
2 Tablespoons peanut butter (natural)
1 tsp. vanilla extract
1/4 tsp. cinnamon

Directions
1. Microwave the peanut butter for 20 seconds.
2. Add yogurt, honey, vanilla extract and cinnamon. Mix well.
3. Dip with sliced apples.

Nutrition Information
Serving size: 4 Tablespoons dip with 1 apple.
Calories: 139
Total fat: 2 g
Total carbohydrates: 30 g
Sugar: 12 g
Protein: 4 g
Sodium: 25 mg

Cucumber and Salmon-topped Crackers

Yield: 4 crackers

Ingredients
12 cucumber slices
4 whole wheat crackers
1/2 cup cream cheese (low fat)
2 Tablespoons cooked salmon (chopped)
1 Tablespoon chives (finely chopped)
1 tsp. red radishes (finely chopped)
1/2 tsp. lime juice

Directions
1. Mix cream cheese with salmon, chives, radishes, lime juice.
2. On each cracker place 3 cucumber slices.
3. Top with cream cheese mixture.

Nutrition Information
Serving size: 1 cracker
Calories: 130
Total fat: 10.9 g
Total carbohydrates: 4.95 g
Sugar: 1.05 g
Protein: 3.55 g
Sodium: 186.7 mg

Carrot Balls

Yield: 10 servings

Ingredients
1 cup almonds
1 cup shredded carrots
1/2 cup golden raisins
1/4 cup walnuts
2 Tablespoons coconut oil
2 tsp. flax seeds
1/2 tsp. stevia powder

Directions
1. Mix all ingredients in food processor.
2. Form 22 balls.
3. Place on a baking tray lined with paper.
4. Freeze for 2 hours.

Nutrition Information
Serving size: 1 ball
Calories: 68
Total fat: 5.3 g
Total carbohydrates: 4.9 g
Sugar: 2.7 g
Protein: 1.6 g
Sodium: 7.4 mg

LOW-SUGAR SNACKS FROM *BEATING SUGAR ADDICTION FOR DUMMIES*

Chocolate Peanut Butter Protein Bars

Yield: 24 bars

Ingredients

2 bars dark chocolate (70% cacao) – approx. 80 grams total
1/2 cup organic milk
1/2 jar (8 oz) creamy organic peanut butter
2 Tablespoons cocoa powder
1/4 cup local honey
3/4 cup organic almond meal
1/2 cup dry uncooked oatmeal (slow cook - not quick oats)
1 cup vanilla or unflavored whey protein powder

Directions

1. In a glass bowl, microwave peanut butter for 90 seconds until it stirs easily. Stir in honey.
2. In a separate bowl, blend together protein powder, oats, almond meal, and cocoa powder.
3. Add protein mix to peanut butter and honey, and mix thoroughly (it will be very thick).
4. Press into 9 x 16 baking pan, approx. one inch thick. Optionally, roll into balls instead.
5. Place baking pan in freezer 5-10 minutes until mix starts to harden a little.

6. In medium saucepan, slowly melt chocolate. When chocolate is melted, remove pan from freezer and coat mix with melted chocolate.
7. Return pan to freezer; remove when chocolate hardens.
8. Cut into 24 servings. Serve at room temperature.

Nutrition Information
Serving size: 1 bar
Calories: 150
Total fat: 9 g
Total carbohydrates: 8 g
Sugar: 3.7 g
Protein: 10 g
Sodium: 67 mg

Three Bean Quinoa Salad

Yield: 6 servings

Ingredients

1 cup organic quinoa
1 can organic black beans, drained and rinsed
1 can organic red beans, drained and rinsed
1 can organic white beans, drained and rinsed
1/4 cup extra virgin olive oil
1/4 cup red wine vinegar
1 teaspoon Italian seasoning
salt and pepper

Directions

1. In medium saucepan, bring 2 cups of water to a boil. Add quinoa, cover, and reduce heat. Simmer approx. 20 minutes until water is absorbed. Remove from heat. Fluff quinoa with a fork.
2. Mix in beans, olive oil, vinegar, and Italian seasoning. Stir well. Salt and pepper to taste.
3. Refrigerate for at least two hours before serving.

Nutrition Information

Serving size: 1 cup
Calories: 296
Total fat: 10 g
Total carbohydrates: 42 g
Sugar: 2.8 g
Protein: 13 g
Fiber: 11 g
Sodium: 450 mg

Turkey Nachos

Yield: 6-8 servings

Ingredients

8 oz ground organic turkey
5 oz organic blue corn chips
1 package taco seasoning mix
4 oz shredded Mexican cheese blend
1 organic tomato, diced
1/2 fresh avocado, diced
1/2 cup chopped onion
1/2 cup chopped organic red pepper
1/2 cup chopped organic green or jalapeño pepper
organic sour cream and/or fresh salsa (optional)

Directions

1. Coat medium skillet with no-stick cooking spray. Combine turkey, onion, and peppers in skillet. Season to taste with taco seasoning.
2. Cook over medium heat until turkey is browned, stirring often.
3. Pile corn chips on large plate. Top with turkey and pepper mix. Sprinkle mixed cheese, tomato, and avocado.
4. Microwave until cheese is melted. Serve warm.

Nutrition Information

Calories: 244
Total fat: 12 g
Total carbohydrates: 19 g
Sugar: 2.2 g
Protein: 14 g
Sodium: 343 mg

Groovy Guacamole

Yield: two 1-cup servings

Ingredients

2 fresh avocados, diced
1/2 cup fresh salsa
1 Tablespoon sour cream or plain greek yogurt
1/4 cup fresh cilantro, chopped
2 Tablespoons fresh lime juice
1 Tablespoon taco seasoning
1 pinch garlic powder
1 cup shredded Monterey jack or pepper jack cheese
Optional: 5 kalamata or black olives, pitted and chopped
salt and pepper

Directions
1. In medium bowl, combine all ingredients and mash together with fork or potato masher. Salt and pepper to taste.

Nutrition Information
Calories: 199
Total fat: 14 g
Total carbohydrates: 11 g
Sugar: 1.4 g
Protein: 10 g
Sodium: 790 mg (with pinch of salt and pepper)

Spinach Quiche Cups

Yield: 8 servings

Ingredients

2 organic eggs
8 oz organic frozen spinach
3/4 cup shredded cheese of choice
1/4 cup organic green pepper, diced
1/4 cup mushrooms, washed and diced
1 teaspoon jalapeño pepper, diced (optional)
salt and pepper

Directions

2. Preheat oven to 350 degrees F. Line 8-cup muffin pan with baking cups greased with no-stick spray.
3. Thaw spinach in microwave (2-3 minutes). Drain excess water.
4. In medium bowl, beat eggs thoroughly. Add spinach, cheese, peppers, and mushrooms. Salt and pepper to taste. Mix well and divide evenly into mixing cups.
5. Bake 20 minutes, until toothpick inserted into center comes out clean.

Nutrition Information

Calories: 78
Total fat: 5 g
Total carbohydrates: 1.5 g
Sugar: 0.4 g
Protein: 5 g
Sodium: 288 mg (with pinch of salt and pepper)

Baby Shrimp Salad with Dill Dressing

Yield: 4 servings

Ingredients

1 pound baby shrimp, peeled and deveined
3/4 cup white wine
2 bay leaves
1 fresh lemon, sliced
3 Tablespoons olive oil
3 Tablespoons red wine vinegar
1 Tablespoon fresh basil, chopped
2 Tablespoons fresh dill, chopped
1/2 medium onion, chopped
1 teaspoon Dijon mustard
salt and pepper

Directions

1. In large saucepan, combine wine, bay leaves, and lemon slices. Fill with water until half full. Bring to a boil over high heat.
2. Add baby shrimp and boil 3-4 minutes until shrimp are pink.
3. Drain in strainer and cool under cold water. Remove bay leaves and lemon pieces.
4. Place shrimp in clean bowl and add dressing (below). Salt and pepper to taste. Toss well. Refrigerate and serve chilled.

Directions for dill dressing
1. In medium bowl, whisk together olive oil, vinegar, basil, dill, mustard, and onion.

Optional: Shake vigorously in a shaker cup instead of whisking in a bowl.

Serving suggestion: Serve on a bed of fresh lettuce, or serve on multi-grain crackers.

Nutrition Information
Calories: 258
Total fat: 12 g
Total carbohydrates: 17 g
Sugar: 3.1 g
Protein: 15 g
Sodium: 833 mg (with pinch of salt and pepper)

Other books from IronRingPublishing.com

Visit **IronRingPublishing.com** to sign up for notifications of new releases, free books, and other special giveaways!

Low Sugar Desserts

by Mary Donovan

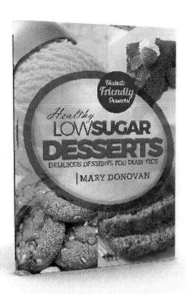

Do you have trouble
keeping your sugar under control?

Are you struggling to lose weight?

LOW SUGAR DESSERTS to the rescue!

Recipe specialist Mary Donovan has prepared a
collection of delicious, low-sugar desserts
especially for diabetics. Inside, you'll find both
cooking and no-cook recipes for you to stay
stocked with healthy, low sugar choices to eat
whenever you need a sweet fix.

BONUS:
The forward is written by Dan DeFigio, bestselling author of Beating Sugar Addiction For Dummies (BeatingSugarAddiction.com). Dan offers both Baking Tips For Diabetics, and a handful of his own favorite low-sugar recipes.

See this and other recipe books at
IronRingPublishing.com

The Two Week Transformation – Lose a pants size in two weeks, guaranteed!

The Two Week Transformation is a simple, straightforward system that will start to change your body in just two weeks.

It's a simple guide that tells you exactly what to do for the next two weeks – what you should (and shouldn't) eat, recommended supplements, exercise tips, and some extra credit options too, if you want to really get serious.

If you follow this two-week plan exactly, you're guaranteed to lose at least one pants size, and you will feel fantastic!

Here's why you'll love *The Two Week Transformation*:

- It's an easy detox plan that DOESN'T involve complicated phases, measuring portions, or starving yourself
- You'll get proven nutrition secrets for maximum fat loss
- You'll be energized and feel great!
- You'll learn how to stop sabotaging yourself and finally find a way to lose weight quickly and easily

Get the kickstart you've been waiting for, andstart your Two Week Transformation right now!

Also available in Spanish!

Disclaimer and Terms of Use

The author and the publisher do not hold any responsibility for errors, omissions, or interpretation of the subject matter herein, and specifically disclaim any responsibility for the safety or appropriateness of any dietary advice or recipe preparation presented in this book. This book is presented for informational purposes only. Always consult a qualified health care practitioner before beginning any dietary regimen or before using any nutrition supplements.

Made in the USA
Columbia, SC
06 December 2019